GET UP
Universal Lessons of Martial Arts

RENSHI LISA MAGIERA

DEDICATION

For Jordan and Nick

CONTENTS

ACKNOWLEDGMENTS

Thank you!

FAMILY: Eric. Jordan. Nick. Anna and Ed. Mary and Jim. Tony. Darlene and Ed.

INSTRUCTORS: Rick. Cliff and Chuck. Beth, John and John. Tony. Jim and Steve. Wayne. Jeff, Bob and Hal.

STUDENTS: Beth. Dominic. Jesse. Madison. Ian. Mallory. Sally. Jay. Kate. Scott and Wilson. Caleb and Ava. Zechariah. Jacob. Emmy and Elsa. Rudy. Jacob. Silas, Sam and Saul. Reannah. Kerri. Trina. Heather. Shawn and Todd. And so many more!

Zizi and Scott. Molly. The Lemonade Stand and WWCR.

LISA MAGIERA

INTRODUCTION

I write like I fight, to the point, nothing extra. Extra costs energy, makes you vulnerable, wastes time, lets the other guy in.

These stories are based on my 20 years as a student and teacher of karate, during which I have observed the attitudes and behaviors of success. The structure is the colored belt system of a martial arts school; the lessons are universal.

You may find yourself asking, "What rank is my attitude? … Am I a creative and rule-breaking blue belt? Or am I a brown belt taking responsibility for my success?

Read it through. It won't take long to get the picture. Return as you please to the lessons of personal mastery that apply to your journey.

SECTION I

WHITE BELT: EXCITED AND EMOTIONAL

I don't remember what we did in my first martial arts class. But I can tell you my impressions: little brown building, skinny hallway, shoes lined up, kids' class ending, canvas mat, adults fixing their uniforms, reverence for the process, respect in the air, feeling nervous, and having one question, *Will I fit in?* I left that day wanting more and that thirst led me on a path to creating the habits of a black belt.

New students are emotional and first impressions will often determine whether they stay or go. Some may quit for the intangible reason, *It just doesn't feel right.* Others don't like the uniform or being barefoot, a person in class smells funny, or they realize that the practice takes work. Hello! "Practice"… "Training." These things imply an investment in time, but let me share the rewards.

You will make friends, the kind who really know you, are fiercely loyal, and are lifelong. You will be challenged to do things you thought were physically impossible and you will succeed. Success in the dojo will translate, like ripples on a pond, into the rest of your life.

Karate is visceral and literal. You will learn how to take a hit and how to counter-attack. Your self-confidence will grow and people won't take advantage of you. If you are afraid, good, go to class anyway. Trust your Sensei to push you to your limits and beyond.

CHAPTER 1 – LOVE IT

"Are you sure you are not a black belt in some other style?"

I grabbed the lapels of Sensei Rick's uniform and said, "No," dropped down onto my right knee, rolled backward and launched him into a flying roll with my left foot.

He soared through the air; my push a compliment to his airborne skill. The flowing garment of his Hakama made crisp circles and his hand slapped the ground.

The sound was satisfying. Throwing a man around: exhilarating.

How had it taken me 25 years to find this?

The invitation was simple. My paramedic friend, Jenanne, said, "I took an Aikido class the other day. The first class is free–I think you'd like it."

I had a busy twenty-something schedule of waiting tables, photographing kids, and volunteering as an EMT, but Sensei Rick taught on multiple days and times. Wherever there was a gap in my schedule, I made time for class. I liked the rituals of lining up, bowing in, meditating, stretching, training on basic techniques, and folding our uniforms before leaving. Practice wasn't work, it was joy.

My growing obsession was apparent one morning during a formal bow to begin training. Sensei Rick watched me struggle to kneel on the canvas mat and asked, "Are you OK?"

I paused before answering, "My back hurts a little."

He raised an eyebrow. "It looks like you can barely move."

"True, but class started at 10." I was wondering how I would get up.

Injury didn't seem like a valid excuse for missing a class, and it hadn't occurred to me that not being able to move would be a problem. After the wrist stretches, Sensei Rick invited me to the side of the mat and performed reflexology on my feet to alleviate my pain. It didn't help, but that was the moment I became hooked on martial arts.

I loved the movement. The constant critiquing and refining of technique made me feel at home. But the individual attention and the care that Sensei Rick showed for me when I was in pain, were something more. I had been wandering and aimless. This felt grounded, respectful, nurturing and deep. It felt like family.

Three months after finding Aikido my job as a portrait photographer moved me from New York to Massachusetts. Anxious to find a new school, I discovered that the style did not matter to me as much as the commute and class times fitting into my schedule.

A cute little old lady who shared her Bible with me when I was church hopping, put her bendy fingers on my leg and explained my challenge perfectly, "As you get older dear, church is less about theology and more about geography."

I found a Korean school with beautiful forms, classes six days and an instructor who honored my training style. Our relationship was pure and simple. He taught. I practiced. He taught me more.

In the 18 months that I trained with Instructor Cliff, before moving to Maine and finding my forever dojo, I developed a crazy work ethic, constant practice of the basics, and a philosophy of molding to and passing over obstacles. Twenty years later, those are the strengths that my black belt is built upon and form the structure that guides my school.

CHAPTER 2 – RESPECT

The day starts early. I take a shower, throw on my gi pants and t-shirt, and wake my husband. The kids are spending the weekend with Grammy, and friends will check on the dog. Eric throws the cooler, our weapons and gear into the hatchback. On time is late. We leave the driveway by 4:30 a.m.

We get to the small town campground and see my instructor setting up music for aerobics. She is the fittest person I know and I am thankful that I do her workouts multiple times per week. I wouldn't want to be any of these people who slept in a soggy tent last night and are just now waking up to a high intensity cardio kickboxing class.

My Sensei is one of those instructors who believes you can rest when you die, and I love her for it. She pushes me harder than anyone else, with a smile and a shake of her long curly dark hair. All too often have I eaten her spinning back kicks, sharpened by a lifetime of hard style Kyokushin karate training.

The music is loud when the class starts and anyone who straggles in after 6:00 a.m. must submit to the 10-pushup entry fee.

Even if it's not karate, the front left side of a class is my spot. My husband Eric is next to me and doing well. He has a few days off from his overnight job with a European car rental agency based in the U.S. This is his awake time, but later he will need a high octane caffeine infusion.

By the end of the first song most of the campers are participating. There are also people sitting on the boulders meant to keep cars off of the grass. Some are parents who feel no need to join in the fun. A few are instructors who have earned the right to skip the morning workout; although most of those are still hotel camping. An unnumbered contingent is recovering from the Saki that flows on Friday nights.

Off to my left is a man I have never seen before. I wonder if he is a part of our group because he is alone. Then I notice his gi pants and large Dunkin' Donuts coffee, which makes me think that he is a Saki survivor.

Instinct guides me to switch spots with Eric, putting him between me and this burly guy until the workout is over.

As we line up for the Saturday morning introductions, Eric and I are joined by other black belts. Our relationship is a mix of tradition and respect, friendship and philosophy.

The informal bow with hands by our sides and bending at the waist is an Eastern tradition, a sign of respect and an agreement to work together to improve ourselves. The American in us shakes hands. If we are more at ease with a person, or have shared in something valuable, we are likely to add a hug.

"Karen!" We bow to each other. We shake hands. We hug.

"Andrea!" Bow, shake, hug.

These are Shihan Wood's students and they have always been at camp. We may only see them for three days a year but we are connected. We live in the same *not quite right in the head* reality.

I take a spot and Chip puts his hand on my shoulder, not a smart thing to do to a black belt, but I look before striking.

"Chip!" Bow, shake, hug.

I notice the guy from earlier is now wearing the camp T-shirt and a black belt. He is joining our line and I ask Karen if she knows who he is.

She tells me, "His name is Dan. He is from away." This is shorthand for a non-Mainer.

"He gives me the creeps." I say.

She nods and starts to say something but is interrupted by Shihan's command to stand at attention and bow in, "Charyut…Kyunyea."

We respond, "Osu!"

He explains the schedule and the rules. This camp is an anomaly in the world of martial arts; Tao Kamp Karate: Where All Styles Share. He welcomes and introduces the instructors who will each present something from their style and expertise. We will train in Kung Fu, Tai Chi, Tae Kwon

Do and Karate. We will learn self-defense techniques, do calisthenics and throw knives and stars.

When he is finished we bow to the instructors and then to Shihan, each time saying, "Osu!"

It is a courtesy, respect for his rank of 6th degree, his years in the arts, and appreciation for his creating the camp. Returning the bow, he shows gratitude for our attendance and dedication.

My first class is with an instructor who holds the title of Renshi, which means polished instructor, and is assigned to black belts in certain Japanese styles who have achieved a minimum rank of 4th degree. He can trace his line of instructors back to Tatsuo Shimabuku, founder of the Isshinryu style.

My school, Bushido Karate Dojo, offers a blend of Isshinryu and Kyokushin Karate. Both are Japanese hard styles and because of the Isshinryu element we were once invited to attend an advanced training workshop at the instructor's pure Isshinryu dojo. At the seminar we were asked about our instructors and were told that they represented a *bastardized version of the art.*

Although I would have gladly practiced further with this man and his pure art I knew that I was not willing to travel to New Jersey from Maine, and submit to the dedication that claiming his line as my instructors would have required. I like my bastardized version for its founders who blended their styles when they married, for their incredible talent and for its flexibility and complexity.

Renshi is short and stalky and standing next to a pile of huge bowling pins. I notice the pins but have no idea what we will do with them.

He introduces himself and tells us, "We will be doing conditioning drills today."

Oh, I think, *that is what the pins are for. This is bad.*

"Grab a partner." He says.

Karen and I jump to face each other. She loves this activity.

Renshi says, "The purpose of conditioning is to kill your nerve endings and make you more ready for battle. One method is to hit yourself against hard objects like rocks, trees, walls, or each other, until you no longer feel it. In the olden days guys used to peel back their skin, sharpen the bones, and then let it heal."

I turn to face Karen and say, "That's gross." She smiles and we begin the first exercise of self-inflicted torture. Our job is to whack our arms against each other in a rhythmic and alternating pattern. The next one is the same basic concept but uses different arm blocks while stepping across the field. Our wrists are red and our forearms are well worked over.

As awful as it might sound, this is karate. It is what we do, and Karen and I laugh our way through the session. We pause to rub down our arms, a superficial attempt to minimize black and blues, and look around to see the other 20 or so black belts moving around under the sun.

Dan is a few yards away working with another big guy. There is something intangibly dangerous about him and a small part of my thinking will be dedicated to knowing where he is at all times today.

Renshi walks back over to the bowling pins. He picks one up, gets in a good front stance and hits himself in the forward leg. He switches his stance and hits the other shin with a little more gusto. Instead of any kind expression of pain he lets out a burst, "Ha!"

We can't help but laugh with him, even though we know that he is demonstrating our fate for the next drill.

He tells us, "Last week I was walking through my house in the middle of the night. I went through the living room and slammed my shin into the corner of the coffee table. I got ready to let loose with a string of swears, then I realized; it didn't hurt. It didn't hurt at all."

There were only four or five bowling pins to be shared by the group. I did what was required, but I didn't like it.

You might say that Renshi's last conditioning drill was a team building event. We made a long curving line, side by side, around the field. Our feet were spread apart in a wide legged squat: kiba dachi, or horse stance.

Like the first drill, this was a person-to-person pain-inflicting process. An Indian sprint of bruising. The person on the end of the line, stood up, faced their neighbor with open hands and dropped straight down into a deep stance, slapping their partner's thighs. They stood up again and moved to the next person, all the way down until it was their turn to rejoin the line.

I was in the middle of the group, standing between my husband and Renshi's wife. Dan was near the beginning and I watched him as he approached us. He was gentle and barely hit the three guys to my left, including Eric.

He slid in front of me, dropped hard and nailed my legs. He did the same to

Renshi's wife, using his full body weight.

What the hell?!

By the time we went around a second time the women were not the only ones retaliating in kind to Dan's aggressive behavior and Renshi made sure that our drill lasted until he had passed through the line a fourth time. I don't know what his legs looked like, but I had hand prints on my thighs for more than a week after that class.

We heard the rumor. Something had happened with the black belts last night—Dan had offended the highest-ranking people in the camp, and instructors had been cleared today to handle it in whatever way they saw fit.

There are some unwritten rules in karate that are not quite as refined as my Nana's *Emily Post* expectations, but they are real. Don't hit a black belt, ever, unless you are willing to be hit back. If you hit a black belt hard expect to be hit back harder, as it is the responsibility of the black belts to create humility in the arrogant student.

Throughout the day Dan was every instructor's "uke." That means that if they had a technique to demonstrate, they did it on him: wrist-melting joint locks, aggressive takedowns, high/low punching combinations, and putting a weapon in his hand and then repeatedly and painfully disarming him.

In the last class of the day we were being instructed by a 9th degree Portuguese Sensei. Hanshi had Dan come forward. "Let's start with Heaven and Earth." As he said it he had Dan punch toward him. Hanshi got under the punch and drove his arm up, grabbed the wrist, twisted it and brought it down past his own waist. The arm bar tossed Dan to the ground in an impressive, *Whoosh*.

Dan stood up easily, the movement was fast but easily managed for an experienced martial artist.

Hanshi said, "Punch again." Dan obliged. "If you can't 'member dat. Try, comb your hair,"…their hands went up… "Tie your shoes…" Dan flew to the ground again.

We spent the next half hour doing a series of moves that all involved the theme of creating movement and momentum by changing directions from high to low, with some wicked wrist twisting and arm bars to control our opponents.

Dan was the sensei's partner for every demonstration. Hanshi wasn't just a part of the upper ranks, he was the upper ranks. He had witnessed what had happened the night before and he showed no mercy to this disrespectful man. During one demonstration Hanshi walked up to Dan and executed a move that is in every Japanese form I know. He grabbed his head with one hand and put a knuckle to his face with the other. Dan dropped like a rag doll.

Holy crap! Did that just happen? I thought. It was the only time I have ever witnessed a pressure point knock out in my career.

Learning to do pressure point techniques involves receiving pressure point techniques. I am certain that I will never perform a takedown like that. I love the beauty in the arts but there is brutality in what we do. Old school, hard core retribution for insults and disrespect are a part of the Tao, the way.

Bu-Shi-Do: Way of the warrior. On the field of battle we must trust the men beside us. We must know their hearts and minds. We must know their location to protect and to be protected. We must act as one to stay alive. There is no room for a man who looks down on another when our mission is to serve. Respect is the foundation of training: silent respect for elders, caring respect for youngers, mutual respect for equals, and a work ethic that shows respect for the knowledge that is shared. A black belt who has not learned to respect is a danger.

Consider the Bonsai architect; he clips branches that do not serve the greater purpose of the art. Dan was clipped that day.

CHAPTER 3 – HUG DEFENSE

Dear Sensei Lisa,

Thank you for all that you and Sensei Eric have done for me in karate…
For the first time ever I took my kids to the mall on my own.
I wasn't scared to do it.
We went to Build a Bear and the kids made their own bears for Christmas.

Thank you again,

Beth

There were plenty of signs. He wasn't original. It was classic abuser stuff. He separated her from family and friends. He controlled her finances. He defended her by beating up other people. They were in a public place when he hit her. She fell to the ground and he started kicking her. No one did anything to help.

They never married but they had a son.

She got away.

There were custody threats and domestic calls; visitation ending with him pushing her up against the wall and stealing her car keys. She escaped with the baby that night and walked home.

He moved away.

Years passed. She married a good guy.

They had 2 sons. She enrolled the oldest in karate when he was 5.

I didn't know anything about her past. But she leaned in. She watched his classes intently. I invited her to join and she said yes.

She cried. She cried before, because she was afraid to come to karate. She cried during class because she was scared and she was having flashbacks. She cried on the way home every night, without exception, for a year.

But she kept coming.

Sensei Jon and I talked everyday about how to keep her safe and moving forward. We were determined not to be her new abusers. We learned when to ignore the tears, when to push and when to stop. We discovered the triggers that would make her panic and freeze.

I have seen women who come to karate for abuse. It can be an acceptable place to receive bruising hand prints on the arms. It seems crazy, but it can be true. They are out there, and they need our help to reframe their thinking.

But that wasn't Beth's story. She wanted to heal, to not be afraid, and she was willing to do the work. She is the most resilient person I know.

Beth had no ego. A person needs confidence to have an ego. She had fear; fear of being in close, fear of being hit, fear of getting hurt, fear of not being good enough, fear of failing, fear of her son getting hurt, fear of men, fear of women, fear of bullying, and fear of losing.

Fear is the most crippling of all emotions. It is intangible and therefor lacks limits to its size and breadth and power over us.

We do very little competition style point fighting in our school. We describe our sparring as, "Slow circular sparring, with both people attacking and defending."

One night Beth was sparring with Sensei Karen. She knew the game, but she was still easily overwhelmed. Karen went faster than Beth could comprehend so she put out her arms and grabbed Karen. She pulled her in and wouldn't let go.

As I looked over, I saw them but I didn't understand what I was looking at. I asked, "Are you guys ... hugging?"

I am sure there were tears on her face when she told me, "I didn't know what else to do."

We still fondly refer to her maneuver as the *Hug Defense*.

SECTION II

YELLOW BELT: CONFIDENCE WITHOUT EXPERIENCE

Getting your first promotion in karate is a big deal, *to you*. It takes a lot of work and it feels good but you may wonder why the advanced ranks aren't more supportive. You are one of them now, aren't you? Well, no you are not. You feel that you are at the top of your game but you don't realize how much more there is to learn.

You are the puppy bouncing happily before the grumpy old dog, who lays down and watches you run laps around the house thinking, *I used to do that, now I know better.*

As a yellow belt you lack big picture thinking, over confident in your limited knowledge. This can get you hurt because you still telegraph your movements, you think too much and your ego makes you exuberant but slow, robotic and clunky to the old dogs in the room.

We are a culture that respects longevity. At BKD an adult brown belt has been training for a minimum of three years, the kids have twice that. In that time they have developed deep friendships with their peers and mentors. They have seen many people come and go in the lower ranks. We do appreciate you, but we are cautious; to join the circle of crossed arms you must prove yourself.

CHAPTER 4 – HUBRIS

I landed at Logan Airport after the sun had gone down. Home was just a train and a bus away, but the busses had stopped for the night. I was living in Arlington at the end of the red line. I had been studying martial arts for about a year. Wearing a jacket, dress slacks, and low heels, towing a suitcase on wheels, I decided that walking the mile home on the bike trail in the dark was a good idea.

I was quite sure that *I could handle myself.*

I practiced static, choreographed, standard wrist lock and cross-grab self-defense moves most nights and my instructor praised my skill and talent. I had never practiced a free-thinking "stun and run" drill in which the attack was a surprise and I had to get away fast. Nor did I realize that the former could get me killed, while the latter could save my life.*

Ahh…The hubris of yellow belt.

I was less than a quarter of the way home before I began apologizing for tempting the Gods with a prayer of, "I am so sorry. What was I thinking? Please don't let me get mugged for being so stupid."

I picked up my pace and mercifully made it home without incident. Lesson learned.

*Few things irritate me more than martial artists who call fine motor techniques that take years of practice to master self-defense. It is not. Stop teaching it as such.

CHAPTER 5 – TAKE RISKS

I can picture Jordan standing by the wall with Beth and the other beginners. One by one I asked each student to come onto the floor and perform our first kata. This big kid stood there, nervous and unwilling, afraid of the critique, afraid to get it wrong, afraid to try, and claiming that he was not smart or capable enough.

That was when he realized I wasn't falling for his crap.

I got right in front of that hanging head, in his space and in his face. I looked up into his eyes, "You can do this. I've seen you do Pinan Shodan. If you mess up I'll help you. Now go!"

Once we laid the groundwork of expectations, Jordan succeeded in the dojo. He and Beth did their 30 minute horse stance on the same night as part of their yellow belt test.

I met Jordan 5 months after his 16th birthday. Four years after his threats to his family got him committed to juvenile detention. He was six feet tall; a black kid in a really white little town. An expert system kid, he could split his staff members, get on or off meds, and punch through walls. We gave him hell for hurting his hand more than the damage he had done to the wall. Big Jordan loved to cook and he gave me hell for having dull knives.

I became a part of his mentoring team. We made decisions, with Jordan, about things like reaching out to his family, finances, a culinary career, and whether he should stay in the system to finish his senior year in high school; which he did at the local public school because he had gotten his act together emotionally and academically.

Team sports and socializing with regular kids were the best parts of high school for Jordan. During his senior year, karate took a back seat to football, basketball, girls, and track.

I sat and talked with him when he ran away from conflict at the dorm, then picked up the phone and told them when he was walking back. I went with him when he visited his, still very fearful, adoptive parents, who continued to keep him away from his biological sister. He cried on the way home. They couldn't "unsee" him as a threat.

I only saw that unstable and hallucinating Jordan once. He was convinced that a gang from New York was on their way to Maine to shoot him. A generous friend who worked in the vocational department at his school credited me, and karate, for him staying on his meds most of the time and breaking his destructive habits.

Kids who are truly broken rarely make it in karate. They can't stand the critical nature of it. Many people, not just the broken ones, take it personally. They can't separate the movement from themselves. They think if the movement is bad, then they are bad. But Jordan didn't take himself too seriously. He was a jokester. He was that guy with the infectious smile. He could kick you in the head and make you laugh about it. He was more than competitive.

Jordan was excited the day we were able to take him to an offsite tournament. Imagine having every move you made monitored by dorm parents and teachers. Now, Sensei Eric and Sensei Lisa are putting you in the van with their family and are taking you to a place where, not only can you fight and not get in trouble, you can bring home a trophy for beating the other guy.

Poor other guy.

He blocked Jordan's foot with his head.

It was beautiful.

Jordan's successes in karate were accumulating. Doing well at the tournament, building friendships, earning praise, developing skill, and gaining rank. A confident young man emerged. But confidence and arrogance are cousins, and ego always leads to stupid.

Eric and I had owned the karate school for three years, and still had a working relationship with our instructors. They are two of the best martial artists I have ever worked with, traditional and hard hitting. In 2007 they each had 30 years of training under their literal and figurative belts.

At a social gathering one evening, a blue belt and a personal friend of our instructors debated the power of attitude and intention with Shihan. He told him, "I believe that if my desire is strong enough that I could beat you regardless of your skills."

Wow! Testosterone and Bailey's make people dumb. Three nights later, Shihan directed the class to, "Get out the mats."

The higher ranks were cautious, aware of the weekend's alcohol-infused conversation. The advanced sparring drill that he set up is a two-on-one fighting scenario. The blue belt was definitely going to be on the mat with Shihan, but who would be the third?

Not me. That was for sure. My instructor had radiated red hot danger all week.

I cringed when Jordan stepped onto the mat. He could kick people in the head. He got a trophy. He was a good fighter. He was taller but lighter than this solid and experienced fighter. He was confident, but he didn't have the experience to understand the whole picture, and it could get him hurt.

Once he stepped on the mat there was no turning back.

Please don't break my student. I thought.

The drill alternates. Shihan was the 'defender.' The blue belt and Jordan were the 'attackers.' Their job was to enter in to throw a punch or a kick. Shihan would block and counter. Doing your best on offense is not a good idea. When I run this exercise I tell my students, "The person in the middle is more amped than you. They have two people attacking. They don't rest in between. Whatever you do, they will react at twice your speed."

Our student and Jordan entered in one at a time. Shihan responded fast, decisive and almost mercilessly. I held my breath when I thought Jordan's long lean leg would snap at the point of impact. It still shocks me that no one got hurt. Indeed, it is a sign of my instructor's superior skill that he was able to use so much force and not hurt them. Incredible!

Often it is the stupid things we do that gain us respect.

I didn't think Jordan would come off the mat unscathed. But he did, and I was proud. It was a black belt moment, a glimmer of the brave man he was to become.

I was frozen by the known, but Jordan was motivated by the unknown. Sometimes being unaware of the real dangers that we face can work to our advantage.

CHAPTER 6 – DON'T COMPARE

Karate is an individual sport in a team environment.

Emmy has just gotten her yellow belt. She is this awesome Swedish-American, competitive, soccer player, wife, business woman and mother of two incredible girls. And she is way focused on getting that next belt.

I want to tell her, "Hold on Emmy! Don't rush. This is a long term thing. It doesn't matter what color your belt is. The color is just a symbol that tells you where to line up. It is not a measure of your ability or your worth. Your athleticism is great, but it doesn't make up for the time it takes to master yourself in this environment."

That is the hardest thing for people to understand. They see that they can do a technique or a kata that someone else struggles with and they wonder, 'Why does that person out-rank me?'

I had a man train with me who used to say, "I don't want to go with the women because I might hurt them." He was mad when I wouldn't test him for brown belt because he thought he was strong and talented. I thought, *If you had the skill and control that you think you have then your partner wouldn't be in danger if you didn't want them to be.*

Gaining rank is not a competition, you are on your own journey with other travelers on the path. People who make it *past* black belt focus less on the color of their belt and more on the process of consistent change and effective learning.

Rank is not a linear thing. It is not a checklist. It is logical but subjective, a culmination of the whole person in relationship to others who have held that position, and the history of the school. You are judged on attitude, current ability compared to your past, knowledge of kata and technical skill, all of which come to life in the way a person spars.

Do you use single concepts or strategic combinations? Are you thinking about every move or trusting your instincts? Can you become a chameleon or do you only have one mode of attack? Left brain logical loves the predictability of memorizing forms while right brain creative thrives on the free thinking fight.

I got hooked on the predictability and structure of martial arts. I was calmed by the repetition that led to deep understanding. Then I fell in love with the physical challenge of the fight. Everything about doing and teaching karate is enhanced by my natural strengths. I feel blessed in every moment in the dojo and have learned to trust even in the biggest mistakes of my career.

Sensei Eric, Sensei Beth and I talk about the best way to reach each student. Emmy is vibrant and capable so it is tempting to leave her alone when there are new students to attend to. But yellow belts are still fragile. She battles with internal demons: A devastating knee injury that took her out of soccer. *Will that happen to me again? What if my job or my kids need me and I can't make time for myself to delve into this in the obsessive way that I know would feel good? What if I don't achieve at the highest level?*

She is a woman who constantly puts pressure on herself to succeed. I told Beth, "She needs us. She needs our feedback to improve. Even if she is ten times better than the person next to her, she needs us to critique her movement and create a challenging environment."

I remember being at that stage. My instructor physically adjusted my hand position while I was doing a two handed archer's block. Even though it was technique she was fixing, I thought, *Wow. She must really like me.*

There is such power in the physical touch; a hand on the back to fix posture, a squeeze of the fist to check pressure or a direct look in the eye will go a long way to grounding her and making her feel valued, welcome and an integral part of our community.

Emmy will make it to black belt. Not because I think she will, but because she possesses the attitude and inner fight to get there. Her daughter is seven and is one of the best blue belts we ever had. They will test for Shodan together and it will be more than just an achievement. They will grow and change together, grapple and struggle, practice and be great friends. Regardless of karate, they share passion and drive in a way that never holds the other back, only pushes them both forward.

It pushes me too, as I realize the part that is mine to play as their teacher.

SECTION III

BLUE BELT: CREATIVE ANARCHY

Dr. Seuss's, <u>Oh The Places You Will Go,</u> has an excellent page for blue belts. It is called the Waiting Place. We call it "Blue belt blues." The quantity of information needed to get to the next level is greater than everything you have done until now. Rewards slow down, excitement diminishes and the real work begins.

Blue belts ask, "WHY?" but they don't listen to the answer. They have been around long enough to know my response and "Because I told you so," is no longer good enough. They must discover their own truth. Martial arts is not linear, academic or verbal. It is in the BODY, different for every person and it must be felt to be real. If a technique does not work then it holds no value.

When a punch gets in: "Damn! That hurt." The block was either done incorrectly or it doesn't work, for you. Change it or get hit again. Blue belts test their limits, choose their weapons, and often return to the teachings that work for them. All students, regardless of their rank, would do well to return to this stage of inquisitive searching throughout their spiraling upward journey.

Karate is awesome for kinesthetic people like me. I do like to talk, but it takes HOURS to process the same crap that can be dealt with in two minutes on the heavy bag. Making contact offers the body a way to receive information. Hitting hard just feels good. *I feel strong. I am powerful. I am in this world. I feel therefore I am.*

Wait. Did she just say hitting *feels good?* Yes I did. Because it does. But deciding when and where it is appropriate is a different conversation, for another time, or book.

CHAPTER 7 – OVER THE WALL

When I ask my students, "What is the best way to get to the next belt?"

I answer their silence with, "By helping the people below you get to yours."

Have you ever seen a bunch of soldiers getting over a wall? What happens? They boost the first two up. Then the most athletic guy kneels down for everyone to step on. The first ones up have great upper body strength, they reach down and help the others over. Finally the man kneeling backs up and sprints at the wall. He leaps, grabs for the guys at the top and they hoist him up. He goes last because he is the most capable of helping everyone else.

Students who make it to black belt do not fixate on their belt color. They do not take a break when they earn a new rank, and they never pass up a chance to help someone else to succeed.

CHAPTER 8 – PLUNGER KATA

"My brother was chasing me through the house with a baseball bat. I ran into the bathroom, came out with the plunger and he ran the other way!"

I never got tired of hearing Sensei Jon tell that story and it was the basis for the philosophy that in a fight, "No one wants to get hit by a dirty plunger!"

The week after sharing that philosophy with the advanced adult class, Sally showed up with 18 brand new plungers.

My instructors always said that, "Pinan Nidan is such a versatile kata you can put any weapon in your hand and make it work."

Nine karate practitioners and thirty-one moves later we had invented the Pinan Plunger Kata. It was an excellent way to immerse ourselves into the form. Did we learn anything significant? Probably not, but we laughed about it and created memories and friendship.

It seemed to me at the time that we were on the fringes of our real training, but I think differently now. Creativity is an essential part of the process of mastery. Sally brought new life into an old form by adding the plungers into our practice.

This same group of people was berated for lack of power and focus in our vertical punches in Seisan kata. We each had between three and five years of training. But there was a gap of twenty years between us and our Isshinryu instructor. Shihan was adamant that we should relax to achieve the snap power he wanted to see.

On a Sunday morning informal practice we worked together to become more powerful. We tried to relax. We increased our speed. We grounded our feet. We punched. We did kata. And nothing felt any different. That hour hadn't changed us. We couldn't get it. Out of pure frustration, we incorporated snapping with our fingers into the form.

We told Shihan that we had been working on the kata, knowing that we had failed in every way to achieve what he was looking for, and showed him our invention. Creative anarchy was our substitution for achievement. He didn't appreciate the joke, and was not impressed.

At that stage in our development true power was a mystery.

CHAPTER 9 – CHASING POWER

Power is a funny thing. The harder you try to obtain it, the more it slips away. Intention is a thought. Thoughts tighten muscles. Tight muscles slow you down. Real power comes from energy moving quickly through the kinetic chain of your body, from ground to strike. Like water moving through a hose, it will get stopped anywhere there is a kink or a bend. The body must relax from joint to joint and yet tighten at the point of impact. Relaxing and thinking are at cross purposes.

Finding your power is like an insomniac getting to sleep.

Advanced students have glimmers of power, but the moment they try to be powerful the concept evades them. The only way a person learns this process is through tens of thousands of repetitions. It is an evolution. It takes at least three years to develop a basic power structure, then another three to refine movement to true non-thinking, wholly accessible speed, focus and fine motor accuracy. Kids take longer because until they stop growing, they lack the physical structure, muscle density and body knowledge to achieve their highest potential.

"How much have you grown this year?" I asked.

"Since January? About 3 inches." Dominic said.

"That explains why you are staying too close to your body with some techniques." It is a phenomenon I have observed many times. "Your brain hasn't figured out that your arms are longer."

I look over my shoulder at the 3 junior black belts practicing with Sensei Eric, Sensei Beth and me and say, "What's next?"

"Empi." Jordan, my daughter, says.

"Hands and feet together. Rei. Slow for Power." I say, as we begin. Kata is the performance of memorized movements to defeat a series of imaginary attackers. This kata uses deep stances with wide open body motion. At slow speed I can see the fine motor mistakes they have: front hand engaged, back hand not fully closed, fleeting tension which causes intermittent power, poor foot placement or incorrect distribution of weight.

"Jesse, your punches are floating instead of hitting a brick wall."

I look at Jordan. "When you strike, pull your arm all the way back, engaging your back muscles."

Then to Dominic, "Don't allow your hand to travel past your shoulder." I demonstrate what he is doing with an open hand strike that travels from my cheek and across the centerline. "When you go too far you exit the place where you had power."

As I look at Sensei Eric his recent work toward his third degree black belt is evident. A group testing date 3 weeks from now is his goal to complete his "Eagle 50." This concept is unique to our school. Every belt rank has required katas. Each student must complete and document fifty repetitions of each one as a part of the test. The test is a process, not an event.

"Drag me to the next rank." I tell them. "When I look at you doing basics make me think, *Wow! Jordan looks like a black belt. What can I do to help her get there?*"

For the past few months, Eric has been training through hurting knees, and a near concussion. He is more than halfway through the 1,100 katas on his list and it shows: The first time through is not practice and he has no memory gaps in our intricate and complicated forms. He continues to uncover finite details within himself making his power fluid and unconscious. Eric's focus and confidence are self-evident and he has a renewed sense of excitement in his teaching.

If I step out and watch then our pace will slow and we all just need to move tonight. Next week we will choose one kata and focus on the bunkai; a pattern of discovery to uncover the purpose of the moves in the kata, but for now it feels good to work.

CHAPTER 10 – PUSH-UPS

I don't get along with Yoga instructors. They yield, I confront; it rarely works out for them.

When the head instructor asked me to punish the advanced kids group for making his yoga instructor cry I laughed until I realized he was serious, then I agreed. I can be old school.

"No games today." I said, as Eric and I put away the bag of cut up belts we had intended to use for flag sparring. It was the end of a karate camp Saturday. We were all melting in the hot sun so I didn't expect much from a bunch of 12 year olds who had been drilling all day. Apparently the yoga instructor came with higher expectations, and had linked the students' behavior to her own emotional baggage.

We tortured them with basics, low stances and attention to the littlest details. We sparred at the end of class and I demanded focus.

"10 pushups for not listening."

"10 pushups for being rude."

"10 pushups for looking away," as they glanced at the 30 foot long golden dragon on 4 foot poles, Bling, that the little kids paraded around us while I was talking.

Finally, I made them each write and deliver an apology to the yoga instructor. Sensei Eric and I hovered as they bowed, extended the note, apologized and shook her hand.

Their punishment was clear, personal, and immediate. I thought it was finished.

Rewarding right action is far superior to public humiliation. But traditional martial arts is like the military; one person's mistake begets punishment for the group and memory is long for any offense. At the close of camp on Sunday the students' poor behavior was addressed again, this time in front of the whole camp.

The head instructor asked the kids, "How many pushups should you do for being rude?" They each had to respond, one at a time. Their answers varied from 10 to 100. "Everyone down." The kids dropped. The instructor didn't realize that the instigators had already left camp.

"Ich! (1)" One of my students was in the group.

"Ni! (2)" I looked up and down the line at the other instructors.

"Son! (3)" I leaned in to the only other female instructor and asked, "Would it be ok to do the pushups with the kids?"

"Chi! (4)" She didn't know.

"Go! (5)" He continued to count.

Then he said, "Ok. Get up."

Oh, thank God!

He was truly merciful, and even though wrongly accused, these good kids did not argue. They were not rude. They accepted the Sensei's teaching. But they were upset and their parents were too. Another instructor and I were caught in the middle.

We all talked about it after camp.

I know my rank. Honoring the most basic karate traditions it was impossible to criticize the head instructor. The kids' behavior was unacceptable to him and it was his camp. He could punish them as he saw fit, but it didn't feel right for who we were as 21st century instructors.

I tried to smooth things over, "You guys are leaders. We expect great things of you. You should take responsibility for your environment. Was there a point where you could have stopped the behaviors of the other kids?"

They all realized that they could have taken positive action. They could have used peer pressure to get the other kids back on track, or they could have approached the yoga instructor after class to support her.

We continued to decompress the situation after the head instructor and the other kids had left the area. I sat under the tent with Eric and our kids, our Kung Fu friends Sifu Banks and Steve, as well as Beth and her son Dominic, who had been in the group.

None of us were happy with what had happened, and we bantered about how we could have handled the situation.

"I wanted to support the kids."

"So did I, but I didn't know how. Could we have done the pushups with them?"

"I was worried that it would be insulting."

"But if we ALL had joined them then it would have shown our support. As a camp we could have shared in the punishment."

"I hated for them to be punished the way they were. But, he wasn't really serious about making them do all of those pushups. He was just making a point."

"I think if just one of us had dropped, the entire camp would've gone too."

"Next time I won't hesitate."

"Me either."

As we were throwing around ideas, Sifu asked Steve to work with Dominic. Martial artists often view their teaching as a gift. Dominic's suffering had earned him some individual training with an instructor whom he greatly admired. It started a lasting relationship not only between teacher and student, but between our schools as well.

Finally we made a new policy: No One Does Pushups Alone. It continues to evolve as a part of our culture. When a person whines, complains or swears in class they have always had to do ten pushups. Drop a weapon and it's twenty. Now, we all submit to the consequences together.

My radKIDS friend, Mr. Steve, doesn't understand. "You martial artists and your pushups." He says.

He's right, pushups as punishment is a not a good teaching tool. That was what we were balking at.

Personal empowerment guru, Tony Robbins, has a philosophy that we are using, called a "Pattern interrupt." Break a cycle of negative behavior and replace it with something more positive. Used properly, pushups disrupt unwanted action and give the offender a moment to reset to a better mental place.

The added benefit to our culture of *No One Does Pushups Alone* is the acknowledgment that we all make mistakes. We support each other. We share the results of our actions and we get better together. My children and the other advanced students cheer, "Yay!" when we do pushups. "We love pushups. They make us stronger."

CHAPTER 11 – STAY BACK

Mallory was a second grader when she and her brother Ian started karate. He was a fourth grader. They attended classes at least twice a week as the fitness portion of their homeschooling schedule. They participated in everything: sleepovers, camps, pajama parties and radKIDS.

Eric and I were certified as instructors for radKIDS, the nationally recognized child safety course. It changed everything. We became better parents because we learned that through building the self-worth of our kids, they would be empowered and capable of making their own good decisions. We became better karate teachers because we learned to teach through the eyes of the child.

Our karate students benefitted because we were able to offer a comprehensive safety course that covered everything from electric outlet safety and dog safety, to how not to get bullied, abused or abducted. The only one able to make a difference when a child is confronted by a person with bad intentions is that child. We teach kids that they are strong and powerful, and that striking certain targets will give them time to get away.

All radKIDS know 3 important rules: First, no one has the right to hurt me, because I am special. Second, I don't have the right to hurt anyone else, including myself, unless someone is trying to hurt me, then I can stop them. And third, if someone does try to hurt me, it's not my fault, so I can tell.

Mallory was the shy, youngest of 6 kids, in an amazing Christian family. She tucked her long red hair into a ponytail for karate. A blue belt after a couple of years of regular attendance, forms practice and sparring, she was still a meek fighter, not looking her opponent in the eye and blocking more than striking.

Her family had just moved to a new home in Mechanic Falls. Mallory was a fourth grader when she was walking home from the neighbor's house...

She could hear people running behind her and she thought to herself, *they must be racing.* As the footsteps got closer she turned around to see a boy coming straight at her. Her trained instinct took over. She put her hands up and yelled, "Stay back!"

He didn't. He threw a punch at her face. Mallory didn't take the time to think, *Why?* She scoop blocked his punch and kicked him in the groin.

I smiled when she told me, "He fell down."

His three friends pushed Mallory into the mud before they ran off. Mallory got up and ran over the railroad tracks all the way to the two family home that her family had just bought and shared with her grandmother, "Nanny."

Victory not a victim. She didn't decide. Her practice decided for her: 1 part karate (the scoop block), and 2 parts radKIDS (yelling 'Stay back!' and the groin kick).

We have all been told to 'practice what you preach.' The reality is that we will 'do what we practice.' In high stress situations we do not make conscious choices. Emotion and instinct take over, but we do not have to be slaves to these.

Mallory's karate training provided her with ongoing and regular combat practice which kept her from freezing in panic. radKIDS gave her the mindset of a survivor and permission to act. The real question to ask yourself is, "What have you been trained to do?"

After the incident Mallory became more confident and more aggressive when sparring in class. An event that had every potential of sowing the seeds of helplessness and fear held no power over a girl who stood up for herself and believed that she was worth protecting.

The week after Mallory was attacked the rest of her family joined karate: Mom, Dad and even her grandmother. Her brother, Ian, and sister were already training with us but Nanny turned out to be the scrappiest of them all.

The boys were never identified, caught or punished, nor did they ever assault that red headed girl again.

SECTION IV

GREEN BELT: TAKE RESPONSIBILITY

Many people stall or quit at the edge of greatness due to attitude, not ability. A person's character manifests in their effort. Effort overcomes skill, over time. A natural ability to move with grace combined with focused drive and powerful execution is the dream, but not the reality for most. Often it is the less "gifted" people who have had to fight for every punch, kick and kata, that are most prepared for the journey of little changes ahead. They are used to the WORK of learning, self-evaluating and adjusting their techniques.

Natural talent might get you to green belt, but the hard workers will catch up to you here. The way forward is to want it and to work for it.

Seek a mentor. Someone who will tell you when you are wrong and has the knowledge and authority to know a better way. Obstacles are abundant: boring repetitions, twice the hours, mental and physical fatigue, and life detours.

Who will stay the course?

CHAPTER 12 – SHOW UP EARLY

As I enter the dojo I bow at the door and look over my glasses to see that Shawn has already arrived and is practicing a weapon kata.

"Nice stances." I say as he looks past his bo staff to see me.

"Thanks, but I can't remember the last two moves."

"Let's start from the beginning." I say as we stand next to each other, bow, and extend our bo staffs forward to begin.

Ten minutes later the rest of the blue belts and green belts begin to arrive. I think to myself, *black belts are made in the 15 minutes before and after class.*

"Kipsu!" The class lines up. Todd bows at the door and rushes to stow his gear bag around the corner before jumping into his place. There are 12 kids here, a slightly uneven mix; Shawn and Todd are the most advanced of the four green belts, both with their sights on brown.

Everyone in the room has things in common: years in, technical knowledge and the ability to combine simple concepts effectively. Everything came a little easier for Todd, who is a natural athlete, lean and strong, smart and able. When Shawn started he was chunky and uncoordinated, and he still has a hard time learning the intricate movements in our memorized forms.

"Get your bo staffs out." I say after our warm up. I know that Shawn needs a few more times through the kata to make it stick and I am happy to bring the whole class along to help him succeed.

I begin to move to the rack but Caleb is standing in front of me with my bo. I look down at him, smile, "Thank you." I say.

"Everyone spread out and face the windows. Left hand down, right hand up." I look around and see Michael standing practically under my right elbow. "Ahh. Get away from me!" I tell him.

He smiles and steps back as I shoot him a look over my glasses and wave him away.

"Shushi No Kon Tao. It is our second Bo kata, if you don't know it just do your best to keep up. Todd, go in the back and Shawn take that spot on the side." I put them on the outskirts so the other kids will have someone to look at when they are facing away from me.

Todd takes his position and I notice his finger extended down the spine of the bo. Rather than embarrass him in front of the lower ranked kids I remind everyone, "Please make sure your hands are tight around the bo. Protect your fingers by gripping it like this." I demonstrate the correct hand position and wander around the room. As I pass Todd, I shift his finger back around the bo into a better position and say just to him, "C'mon, I shouldn't have to say it more than once." What was acceptable at blue belt, is not anymore, he has to fix it. Respecting me enough to follow directions and having the mindfulness to execute correct form are equally important now.

At this rank it is the details that need adjusting for a student to progress from green to brown belt. Sure they have to learn new and more challenging katas but that is somehow irrelevant. There is always new stuff to learn. The real question is: Do they want it, really want it?

We repeat the weapons form four times and it is time to split the class. Shawn takes my bo from me and I ask, "How's it feel? Got it?"

"I think so. Thank you Renshi."

"My pleasure." I feel more confident about Shawn's path than Todd's.

He has overcome injury, his weight, and scheduling conflicts. Todd's parents have been dedicated to his success from the beginning, but he has never taken over that responsibility. He has the skill to advance to brown belt, but unless he becomes more personally invested, mastery of the arts will always evade him.

It is just too much work to get to black belt unless you are committed, all in and can't live without the training. Brown belt is hard work. Shawn has been wise to seek me as his mentor. The Jr. black belts have invited Todd to join their weekend morning routine, but he doesn't yet realize the impact of surrounding himself with higher ranked people, and hasn't shown up.

"You know what I love about karate?" They freeze in their stances and reply together, "No, Renshi!"

"I love that it happens from the tips of your toes to the top of your head!" To this I receive some confused stares, but no rolled eyes. They know better. "Most of you are doing an excellent job with the forward hand, but because you are learning a new weapon kata you are forgetting the back hand and other basic pieces are falling apart. Stances! Show me a good cat stance."

"You have to bring your good foundation with you into the hard stuff. If you can learn something new and have good stances and good hand positions then the memorization goes faster. Repetition is king." They are still looking at me funny. I might as well shock them.

"Of all the stances, a cat stance can save your life!" I choose my victim. Caleb is sturdy and doesn't scare easily. I run at him and yell, "Ahh!" He jumps back and loses his balance.

"Aha! If you had used a cat stance you would have been ready to change direction and fight back if necessary. Could—have—saved—your—life— Caleb." I say leaning over him with a big smile on my face. "I totally had you. Dead. Definitely dead."

Everyone laughs and I decide to move on from bo training. I have been frustrated with the class's stances lately. Today is the day to deal with that. "Put your bos down in front of you." I say. The staffs are laid down with a light clatter. I put my feet together and look out at this great crew of kids. "Put your feet together in a V. Heels touching. Sit down as far as you can by bending at the knees." They join me in the beginning stage of a cat stance. "Backs straight. Lower. Now stay. You should feel your heels pressing together." I stretch out my arms but the rest of my body sinks downward. "Let's just stay here for one minute."

Fifty-five seconds later I say, "Stay down. 5. 4. 3. 2… Don't get up! Look down at your feet. See your left big toe? Good. Now take the heel of your left foot and place it where the toe was, foot down straight ahead, and lift the heel. Sink down—ahh—no popping up.

"Niko Achi Dachi. Cat stance. Eyes forward. Guard up." We raise our hands in front of our bodies. We spend the next twenty minutes going through the five stances: attention stance, horse stance, cat stance, front and back stance. We alternate sides, stay low and embrace the concept that, "Lactic acid is your friend!"

Shawn looks straight ahead, legs shaking and hands just slightly out of position. If I go over I will have to break my stance so I log it for later and survey the rest of the class. Rodney is floppy and standing almost straight up, but he was on time for class today and is engaged, which is good for him, so not a concern. Todd is in a good stance but he is looking at the mirror off to his right. If I was standing near him I would push him over from his blind side.

It makes me crazy that a kid with such ability just doesn't try. Shawn has almost caught up to him in technical ability. It is hard to quantify desire, but Shawn just wants it more. Last week his mom said, "Every morning before school he is at the bus stop practicing his katas."

I demand respect from my students, but respect that is given, not taken, is far more valuable. Passion for the art is an inward focus that manifests in perseverance, an indomitable spirit and personal accountability.

I tell the class, "Kokutsu dachi." Todd drops into a perfectly balanced back stance, legs bent, guard up, torso twisted slightly to the front of the stance. He is a natural technician.

"Jump and switch."

"Mawate!" We switch again.

"This time all the way around." Shawn and I do a hop before we turn. Todd makes it look easy: hanging air time, guard up and legs bent on the landing.

When the pressure is on he will lower his stances and show off great form. He usually beats Shawn at our tournaments. Four years from now they would make a great teaching team; one the technician the other a compassionate and empathetic guide for the kids who struggle.

I battle with Todd about that finger position. I battle with myself as a teacher on how to reach him, *Does he just not care? Should I use punishment when encouragement doesn't work? Unchanged, those details will keep him from black belt. Have I provided him with enough obstacles so that he will endure the coming challenges?*

Legs shaking, we finish working on our stances. "Let's split up into two groups. Sensei Eric, you take the blue belts. I will work with the green belts."

I stay on the far side of the dojo, away from the parents. The green belts join me. "Let's talk about attitude." I tell them. "You guys have great skills. You have been training for a long time. You know what I expect from you, but getting to brown belt is all about what you expect from yourself. The single biggest thing you need to do is to take responsibility for your success."

"No more blaming mom for getting you here late. If you had your gi on and were waiting by the door five minutes before it was time to leave would you ever be late for class?" I ask, singeing Todd with my eyes.

He says, "No, Renshi."

"Here's what I think. Green belts blame other people for their failures, but brown belts don't. They figure out what needs to be done, and they do it. Can you guys do that for me?"

"Yes, Renshi." They say in unison.

"Awesome! Let's do Chinto. It is the last empty handed kata you need for brown belt."

Their eyes light up at the mention of this elusive form that is interesting, challenging and required. "Todd, go in the back. No. Over there so we are all in a diagonal line. Hands and feet together. Rei."

He nods, and we have an understanding. I respect his ability and am happy to put him in a leadership position. I hope he makes it. He is a great kid, talented and capable, but is he driven enough? Shawn has been arriving early for class for the last month and I have seen his knowledge grow. He has overcome much in this journey and that has prepared him mentally.

I believe they will both make it to brown belt, but black belt rank may take another 3-6 years. I have given up taking it personally when people quit. Of these four kids we will lose at least two. Their family could move, an injury might take them out, another sport may draw their attention, finances could change or they could just stop loving it.

My hope is that our relationship and their passion will both continue to grow. Karate schools don't just hire people off the street. These guys are my future in karate as much as I am theirs.

CHAPTER 13 – PRACTICE

"Are you sure that's the right color?" Glenn asked as I was about to place a blue belt with a black stripe on Julie's waist. He is one of the staff members that does karate with his clients.

I considered his question and respected his keen observation. I threw the belt that I had in my hands over my shoulder, turned and approached the belt rack on the wall. Sensei Eric's belts were displayed there. I reached up and grabbed the green one.

"Julie, you are an amazing student." I looked into her twinkling eyes and waited for the smile to reach them. She is in her twenties and has Down Syndrome. "You have taught me to be a better teacher. And I think you practice your katas more than anyone I know."

I tell the group who has gathered for the promotions of Julie and her peers, "Something you should know about Julie is that she calls me on the weekends. The phone will ring … 'Hi Sensei. I am confused. Which way should I turn in Seiuchin?'" I look over at her petite mom sitting with arms and legs crossed and plead: "May I please have a drawing of her bedroom?"

"Julie, you practice all the time and it shows. By yourself, you just performed all four of the katas that I have taught you, and you did them beautifully." (The rest of the group had needed a helper to get through the first three katas.)

"Take off that blue belt." She fumbles and I reach in, take off her blue belt, fold it in half and place it around her shoulders. I replace it with the green belt and tell her, "I will order you your own green belt but you can wear Sensei Eric's until it comes in. I am so proud of you!"

We hug and everyone claps and cheers for Julie.

Karate is an individual sport in a team environment. Our normal green belt standard is 8 katas for both kids and adults. But in this group, Julie's 4 katas were exemplary. I have to give Glenn the credit for recognizing the spirit of the moment. He trains beside them, respects their individuality and is an excellent advocate.

Julie has transitioned to the regular teen/adult class at BKD. Last spring she received her brown belt (There is a video about her test at www.RenshiLisa.com), with 10 of the 12 typically required katas. She is catching up. The Jr. black belt system will give her time to master the rest of the list.

I know that Julie is capable of the skills of a black belt. She is amazing. She can do the techniques and combinations that I ask of her. She has proven that she can learn forms. In time she could test for her black belt with all 14 empty hand and 4 weapon katas.

But will she make it to black belt?

There are two types of students: Those who disappear after a belt test and those who come more.

Julie has disappeared. Fear has gripped her—inner demons and a lifetime of labels bearing their fruit. I ask that you pray for her, that God would take her fears and transform them into motivation. Every day is a battle. Together we can be victorious. But first, you have to come back to class.

CHAPTER 14 – FIGHT

I grab the edges of the metal face mask attached to her helmet. In spite of the tears streaming down Beth's face, I pull her in closer.

"You are worth protecting."

She tries to pull away, but I hold on, my forehead now touching the cage.

"Yes, you are."

She fumbles with the hockey glove on her hand, the pad on her elbow.

"Look at me. You can do this."

Beth shakes her head side to side as I release my hands and turn her by the elbow. We look across the dojo floor at my husband. To Beth he is seven feet tall right now. The head to toe padded foam of the "Red Man" suit does that. It transforms a normal guy into the perpetrator of your nightmares.

Deep fears rumble to the surface. Two years of karate training turn to ash. She trembles as I finish giving her directions.

Beth turns away from Eric and closes her eyes, gulping in short stuttered breaths. I look over her shoulder to my husband. Silently I say, "Now."

Eric does that hulk thing with his arms as he approaches us. "Hey baby. I hear you're pretty good."

She is not allowed to move until he touches her.

"Come with me. Let's go for a ride." He leans in, just inches from her head. Like corduroys, the dipped foam sound of the suit reveals his closeness.

"Tell him to stay back. Use your voice."

Her command is barely audible.

"C'mon Beth. Louder." The volume goes up to a 2.

The three of us are in the same breathing space. I back up a step; look over her shoulder and into Eric's eyes and nod.

Beth is not here in the safety of the dojo right now. She is being restrained by her baby's father, praying for the cops to get there.

Fight? Flight? Freeze?

Act or Die.

Beth's puffy red eyes open, she sucks in a breath and I can see the panic on her face.

She chooses freeze. I choose fight. "Stomp on his foot. High elbow. Again. Low hammer fist."

A visible distance exists between the sound of my voice, her brain, and her body. The disconnect results in a lack of conviction, but she is moving, acting out the moves that could have kept her from falling on the floor.

Eric plays his role with compassion, slowly loosening his grip as he pretends to feel the shots to his head and body. The tight circle of his arms eventually opens on the outer edge.

"Run!" I yell.

Beth falters slightly as we escape to the doorway.

Reaching for a fist bump I say, "Nice! Let's do it again."

"No."

"Yes."

"No."

"You can do better. Let's go."

"I don't want to." She is defiant.

"You are going again."

She grumbles.

I smile.

As our dispute ends, I guide her back to our starting position. She's crying again. I grab both of her gloves and tell her to close her eyes.

When I release her the red beast is moving swiftly toward us. He slides around her and I step back.

Beth's eyes fly open as he lifts her off the ground, this time face to face.

She pauses. I open my mouth to make a suggestion, but it is not needed.

Beth screams, "NO!" She kicks him hard.

Eric's choice to leave her arms free is the cause for an untouchable headache that lasts for three days.

It all happens so fast that I am left with the weight in my heels. I rock forward and chase after Beth running out of the room. She stops at the top of the stairs.

"Get this thing off me!" I grab the chin strap to the claustrophobic head gear and do as she commands.

CHAPTER 15 – STAY LATE

Sarah arrived at what she thought was the beginning of an invitation-only training, an hour late. The look she gave me said it all, *Why didn't you call me to tell me the time had changed?*

I thought, *Why weren't you in class last night so I didn't have to?*

We had a good day with our Isshinryu friends. Sarah left at the appointed time. Eric and I are always the last ones to leave an event. We stayed and talked with Renshi (the bowling pin to the shin guy). He had no sympathy. "The people in the room know the information. It is not our job to chase them."

Wow! That was a different perspective than I was used to having with my *Let's please all of the customers all of the time no matter the cost to our own personal energetic reserves* mentality. That was in my 30's. I no longer possess that instinct or desire it to return.

Eric and I always say, "The real learning happens when class is over."

We stay up late when instructors arrive the night before a camp or workshop. We discuss how best to reach our students, what we think they need and we debate the standards for belt rank promotions. We go to lunch with the Sifus after karate camp, reflecting on the weekend and sharing the history of the instructors. We linger at business meetings to watch, listen and participate with the experts in the room.

You weren't there. I have no obligation to share those lessons with you. But stay after the class, the meeting, and the conference and I guarantee that something of higher value will emerge when people are relaxed, open and are reflecting on the day's events.

SECTION V

BROWN BELT: POWER STRUGGLE

Brown belt is an advanced rank and it is difficult to exit this stage. Techniques must be changed, old habits released, and the tiny, detailed refinements that make the biggest impact to overall success are hard to make.

If mastery has a midway point then attaining brown belt is the beginning of the second half of that journey. We recognize it as a teaching rank but a student will spend just as long here as they did in the lower ranks. Refining technique is the goal. It is a more arduous process than learning basic movements. It requires the student to evaluate and adjust methods that he already considers correct.

The physical movement, thought processes, and work ethic that were used to gain this rank may not apply anymore. Brown belts know the rules and the basis of the game but they have yet to see beyond themselves. Recognition as a skilled player is often accompanied by wavering confidence. Whatever fears have not been addressed thus far will rise to the surface at brown belt.

CHAPTER 16 – HAVE FEAR

I can hear the child crying. I turn to go up the stairs and a small voice says, *These are not my stairs.* I cannot ignore the sound, so I begin to climb. On the fourth step I think the electricity has gone out. But my inner wiring causes the malfunction. My vision is gone. I reach for the banister and haul myself up the stairs.

The sound is to the right. I feel my way toward it. There is a wall, then a bookcase and a light switch. I try the light. When it responds I am shocked to find myself on a dirt road between two buildings.

I cannot hear the baby crying.

There is a man running toward me. *Is that—Indiana Jones?*

"C'mon." He says grabbing my arm. Before I turn I see four guys come around the corner after him at top speed. We run out of the alley together.

I stumble as we cut hard to the left and duck under the vibrant colored cloth hanging at an outdoor shop. Accosted by the aroma of spicy meat on an open fire, I pull up short behind my childhood hero with two sturdy men blocking our way.

There's gonna be a fight. Instinct tells me.

Indi reaches for his whip, but it's not there. I yell, "Hey!" and toss it to him. He circles it around his head to keep the men, dressed in all black, standing before us at a distance and I turn to face the four.

The ground has softened. It sucks me in up to my knees. I try to lift my arms. No response. *Oh Please. Oh please. Oh please. How many chances do you get to fight with Harrison Ford? He's even wearing the hat! The best I can do is freeze? Ugh!*

I hear the baby crying again. It is close. It is mine. *Wake up!*

Jordan is done napping, and so am I. *Why am I so tired today?*

I drag myself off the couch and over to the crib, where she is standing and reaching for me. "Okay, buddy. Let's go for a walk before dinner."

After her favorite "No argument food" of macaroni and cheese, we sneak into Eric's daytime cave and wake him up so that I can go to karate.

Teach two and take two; that is my schedule every Tuesday and Thursday from 3:30-8:00 pm. I take solace in the fact that I regularly do 4 hours of martial arts. In three weeks I test for my black belt. It is only scheduled for three hours. *How hard can it be?* Gulp.

My instructors have been pushing me, and tonight is no different. "Grab a partner." Sensei says, and Shihan steps in front of me. "The person moving forward punches. The defender steps back and scoop blocks." She demonstrates with Senpai Emily, who is equal to her size.

Shihan outweighs me by 60 pounds. His forearms are the size of my biceps. My back is to the wall, so I punch first as we move across the floor in a straight line. He blocks as if I do not exist. I am a bug landing on his sledge hammer arm.

"Mawate." We switch directions. Shihan drills me with his punches. I do the technique as my Sensei directed only once. His thick conditioned white knuckles grazing my chin as I lean back and suck in a breath.

Tapping with the other arm, and side stepping as I move backwards is my only chance keep him off. The count is fast for my added movement but he doesn't correct me so I stay with it until my back foot brushes the wall behind me.

I have not been looking at Shihan's face to read his expression. His head isn't going to jump off his shoulders and strike me so there is no need. I glance up when we stop. I don't see pride. I don't see disappointment. I never can tell what they think. I want to please them but always sense that my best efforts miss the mark.

"Bow to your partner." Sensei directs the class to switch partners. We rotate through more basic scenarios that travel in straight lines.

Sensei says, "Yamae!" to stop the last drill. "Now, stay with your partner. Both people attack. Both people defend. Slow, circular sparring."

My partner is the Sensei John. He is a good friend, my size, and I trust him. There is genuine respect between us. But damn that double kick of his! He gets me with it every time…tonight is no different. "Ugh." I grunt, then add, "Os!" to politely acknowledge the shot to my solar plexus—again.

John smiles, chuckles at me, and bats away my fast flurry of punches. Sensie says, "Yamae! Stop. Switch partners."

I bow out with John and in with Larry. Larry and his daughter have trained together at BKD for 8 years. He usually keeps me out of range with his long legs. Something is changing within me. Test is coming up. I am sick of getting hit. A voice inside says, *Get in close*. Nothing else has worked so I trust, and I go.

I duck inside as a kick targets my head. I punch. I punch fast. I punch a lot. Larry is so used to me backing away from his kicks that he gets flustered and stops.

We all have our own language, communicating in predictable ways. I shocked Larry with my new vocabulary of in-close fighting. He stopped for maybe a second, then renewed his attack. But there was a new wariness for me. Was it respect? Who knows? I was an invader to their camp. Everyone in the room had so much more time together in the dojo than I would ever catch up to.

We switch partners. I am with Shihan again.

I feel like I am going to die. He towers over me. Drives me back. Overpowers with every punch and every touch. I can find no defense against this man. I cower and burst into tears. We are near the back of the room and I find myself in the closet, crying uncontrollably. He is not impressed. I feel the disappointment flow over me. Why are they promoting this weak spirited person to their coveted black belt?

How will I handle a black belt test if I can't handle a little sparring with my instructor? Why am I breaking down? Why am I so scared? And so emotional?

The answer became clearer in a few days, than it was when I was huddled in the closet with the kicking shields. I was pregnant.

Tears shut things down. They are the woman's fail-safe. My baby sensed danger and sent the "freak out" emotions to handle the situation. Disable the situation and get me, us, out of harm's way. It was embarrassing, but it worked.

After I tested for black belt a few weeks later, bold and inappropriate, one of the black belts asked me; "After you have the baby are you going to do the sparring portion of the test?"

Great. More doubt. More fear. It would take me years to feel like I really deserved the rank, years of owning the school. Thousands of hours of teaching every class: Fitness, Kids and Adult karate—30+ classes every week. These days I have no doubts about my rank. I have put in my time. I am immersed. There is no separating me from the arts or karate from me. I am all in, all the time, unsure of who I would be without the dojo, the title, the students, the events, the family, the respect, the love, the movement, the injuries, the school.

Whatever has transpired has been my doing. I am wholly and completely responsible, with the grace of God, for the results of my choices. I am forever grateful to Shihan Beth and Shihan John for passing their school on to me, to Sensei John Shrader for believing in me and teaching with me, for my amazing husband Eric and his support of all of my crazy, for Sensei Beth Adams for everything, especially early morning workouts, for Jordan and Nick for not having the choice and loving it anyway, and for my thousands of incredible students.

Follow your fears. They are set before you to be overcome. Have faith. Seek support. Take action. Fail. Repeat.

CHAPTER 17 – BE OVERWHELMED

Sifu told Dominic that he was a light-foot monkey. If a Kung Fu master really likes you, he will lean in and assign you a monkey. I got drunken, like Sifu's specialty, but I am not sure I have lived up to the name. One style of martial arts is a lifetime of training. Two is a commitment beyond my capacity. That said, I will steal as much as I can whenever we train together.

Dominic has developed his groundedness in karate but still maintains that signature springy motion of his monkey. He practices whatever Sifu gives to him and does so with my blessing.

The "No One Does Push Ups Alone" weekend was the start of an ongoing practice for Dominic with the Sifus. He is the perfect student. He appreciates their teaching. He practices what they give him, earning the right to new knowledge. They value each other in a way that a payment system involving dollars rarely produces.

We are told that Sifu means brother; family is an appropriate analogy for my martial arts community.

When Dominic was preparing to test for his brown belt I wanted to support this relationship, so we scheduled his test for the same weekend as our Monkey Kung Fu winter workshop. Instead of a normal concentrated test, we considered spreading it throughout the day, but Dominic's dad had to go to work and couldn't stay.

Parents matter to me. I always choose to have mom and dad in the room, whenever possible, except for the black belt test.

Dominic had demonstrated his katas, plus Gate Keeper, a Kung Fu form that Sifu had assigned to him. My plan was to do the sparring at the end of the day, but his dad had to leave. In the middle of discussing with Eric and Beth what we should do, I made the decision. I stopped mid-sentence, rushed across the floor, reached out with my left hand to grab his right arm and raised my right hand to punch and yelled at Dominic, "Fight!"

Dominic looked up at me and backed up as he tried to defend against the assault. He did well, but later, when I saw the photos, I realized how shocked he and the onlookers were.

Sparring is a part of what we do. It is normal to us, but parents and friends rarely get it. My mom hates watching her grandkids spar. What feels fun and exciting to us, looks aggressive and violent to her.

Dominic was 5 when he started. He has grown up in the dojo and is a talented martial artist. This test was all about raising his confidence and ability to a new level and for that he would need to be challenged in a way that he had not experienced before.

Teenagers are wonky. Yes, I said wonky. Here is this long limbed kid, who has grown 6 inches in twice as many months. His reach has increased but his brain hasn't figured out the math yet. How far do his punches and kicks reach? It is all still in progress.

Dominic cried. He was overwhelmed as the attack charged and then changed from me to Eric, to Beth (his mom) and back to me. Sifu Steve was on the side and he tucked him under a shoulder at one point to encourage him.

The whole thing is a classic game of good cop / bad cop. All of us with the same goal in mind: to take the potential we see under the surface and help our student to, not only discover it, but to use it. Belief comes through action.

The speed of our techniques creates the illusion of danger. Ok, if he misses the blocks and we are trying to hit him then he could be badly injured. I punch hard, I kick hard and I am not afraid to touch, but my intent is not to hurt a 13 year old kid who is my best friend's son, and whom I have trained for 8 years. Do I want to challenge him? Yes. Am I willing to scare him? Absolutely. Am I able to pull back if he falters and misses a block? Of course, that is my job.

The overload principle is a straightforward concept in fitness. You must overload the muscle, bring it to the point of imminent failure. In fact, the greatest growth is produced by pushing the muscle past the point of failure.

Karate is the same. Dominic did very well in his test. He was emotional, but I have never seen that reaction since. Success in the midst of adversity has allowed him to overcome his instinctive response of fear, and replace it with confidence and purposeful action.

CHAPTER 18 – SEE THE BOARD

Sparring with Sifu is my favorite thing to do at camp. He is fast, versatile, flexible, and strategic. There is no time for thinking. Adrenaline is my friend, conscious effort my enemy.

Lessons come later, as fleeting memories knit back together. I wake up in the night, 10 hours after sparring with him and realize things like: *Why did I let him distract me with that grab to my arm? I should have ignored it and taken advantage of—Well, who am I kidding, I wouldn't take advantage but next time we spar, 6 months from now, I'll ignore that grab.*

Ten minutes before the first session of Karate Camp. I see my chance. Sifu is watching his students warm up with bo staffs.

I run across the field, tossing my sunglasses as I go. Better to take them off myself because we fight close. Sifu turns and assumes a fighting stance: back leg weighted, hands open and relaxed, palms slightly up. His arms extend to meet my onslaught. I've lost the advantage of surprise; it might have been the running, more ninja next time would be good. I throw a punch. It doesn't matter where we start. This un-choreographed dance will spiral and loop in multiple directions, fluid action creating space for unplanned reaction.

No one fights me like Sifu. We train in different arts. His Shaolin techniques mold and adapt to my hard-style blend of Isshinryu and Kyokushin. Our movements have become less surprising and different to each other after years of play.

Sifu Banks has twice my martial arts experience, yet he is without ego, a willing teacher who takes two steps every time I take one.

One strike will not end this conversation between old friends. It meanders around as we express our opinions and try to outwit the other.

A kick that reaches in is cause for celebration, *Yay!* It is brief as his response is immediate, twice what I have done, and taking advantage of the very thing that I imagined doing well. *Damn.*

This game we play is a chess match, patient, fluid and ongoing. I fixate on the piece. He sees the board. I go straight. He goes in circles. I circle. He straightens. I strike hard. He wraps around me like water surrounding a rock in the rapids.

Drunken wants you to think he is off balance. Distraction and deception; that is his game. Almost falling over, he is at his fastest, strongest and most dangerous. I know that when he seems off balance I should worry, but the old slow mind of assumptions betrays me.

Dangerous in the play is a touch, a knowing glance that *I got you.* A nod of acknowledgment by the other and the movement continues. These days I feel flesh under the flowing garment of the master. It wasn't always that way.

Success is short lived, while the response is harder and more painful than it used to be. Teacher telling student, *Oh, so you think you got in? I was being nice. I allowed it.*

Getting hit hard by your instructor? It means you are doing well, unless he is just being a jerk. The relationship outside the fight is reflected inside.

A couple of years ago Sifu told me I could come down off the mountain, proud instructor releasing his student to fly on her own.

This is me wanting back up on that ledge of predictability and safety. This new stuff is scary and hard and it hurts. *Please can we return to the mountain?*

He grabs. I do not resist this time. No time to take notice. Later tonight I will realize how great that is, but I am immersed. Trusting my own movement. Think less. Move more.

I strike over his extended arm. He leans away, giving up nothing in position. A touch to the back of my head. I nod. He is high, I go low. He is over me now and we are rolling. Doesn't mean it's over, just relocating.

On the ground I extend my leg to push him away. Never losing balance he takes a step back. He inclines his head, extends a hand to me and we are standing in the middle of a crowd.

SECTION VI

BLACK BELT: SURVIVAL

"Are you a black belt?" It is the first question people ask when I make the statement, "I own a karate school and a fitness center." It is a loaded question, full of assumptions like, "I bet you could kick my ..." and lacking perspective. Would you make that statement to a person with a dual master's degree in psychology and physical fitness? Probably not.

Becoming a black belt is a process. Shodan or first degree black belt, in my school represents, over a thousand hours of training. It is a bachelor's degree in pursuit of oneself and no one makes it without absolute conviction and love of the arts.

Inner drive overcomes injury, life circumstances, naysayers, schedules and personality conflicts. But the world must also collide in a way to make success possible. For those who do not make it, obstacles appear insurmountable. For those who do, the same road blocks may go unnoticed.

As a teacher I place challenges in the paths of my students at the right time.

Perseverance can be learned. An attitude of mental toughness can be encouraged, but it is messy work. It involves fear, and crying, and pushing students to the edge of what they believe is possible, then pushing a little further.

I have experienced the joys and hardships of this combat sport and I would not live without it. It is hard, honest, brutal, brilliant and life-changing.

CHAPTER 19 – GET UP

Moms who don't do karate, don't like to watch their kids spar. Eric's mom sat at the bottom of the dojo stairs during the sparring portion of his black belt test. Trina and Eric were sparring simultaneously with different partners as his mom listened to the sounds from above.

She imagined everything to be related to her son. She was horrified by the thud of a body being thrown to the ground followed by a repeated chorus of, "Get up!"

I was there. The thuds were impressive, one of them breaking Trina's foot.

She hid the injury, the test nearly over. When Shihan Beth asked Trina to break a board with a kick she didn't hesitate, using the injured foot because she couldn't balance on it long enough to kick with the other.

Eric came to the test with a sprained ankle and endured the entire thing. They both passed and Eric joined me as a black belt.

Months later I was driving down the road distracted by the tears and sobs of some life situation. I don't remember the situation, but I do remember what pulled me out of it. I started asking myself questions: *Are you gonna let this beat you? No.*

I pictured that team of black belts bringing Eric and Trina through their test, encouraging them to "Get up!" and I asked another question: *Are you gonna get up? I don't know, this is hard… Are you gonna lay down and quit? No.* I paused and asked again. *Are you gonna get up? Yes.*

CHAPTER 20 – SLAY YOUR DEMONS

Sensei Eric easily keeps Beth at arm's reach, like a big brother taunting his kid sister. He reaches out and taps her on the head. She manages to kick him with the ball of her foot, then punch him in the ribs. He leans back and chuckles.

I hate it when he does that. "Get him Beth." I say.

We are two hours into Beth's black belt test. Beth has demonstrated her proficiency in basic techniques, forms, and weapons. Now it is time to fight. She is the only one testing today, which means there are no breaks: physically, mentally or emotionally.

I give the command, "Yamae! Stop." followed by, "Beth, you are my partner. Sensei, put on the suit."

Eric moves toward the closet to get his gear on.

Beth doesn't have time to watch him. I escalate the fight. Fighting her is like fighting myself. Our punches are equally fast and accurate, the ball of her foot equal to my heel, but I am not as tired as she is.

Tired is my goal for her, preferably exhausted. Beyond thinking, on the verge of panic is fine. Adrenaline keeps you alive, but only for so long. Today we seek a deeper reservoir.

I bow out and invite Sifu Steve to take my place.

Soft style practitioners are the close talkers of martial arts. He does not hit like we do but his proximity is frustrating and depletes her reserve. Her offense breaks down as she tries to keep him off.

Next is Hal. Before he goes I pull him aside. I remind him, "She hates to be taken to the ground, but that is what we need right now." He is a big guy and she is a little woman.

He bows to Beth. She bows to him. She puts her guard up and is immediately thrown to the ground. Shaken, she gets up. He grabs her again and throws her off balance before getting a good grip and bringing her down again.

I trust these men implicitly. They are talented and selfless martial artists. Otherwise they wouldn't be at Beth's test. The test is not for me, for the school, or for them. It is for her. She has demons to face and it is our responsibility to bring them to life for her.

Tears fill her eyes. Defeat seems imminent.

This is my friend, my student, and a woman who has been beaten down by circumstances, crappy relationships and life. We have avoided putting her on the ground for years; 4 nights per week for 6 years to be accurate. It is her biggest trigger for tears, panic and flashbacks. But not today.

Today Beth will win. She will win on her terms and in her time, but she will win. We won't be done until she does.

Screw talk therapy. Screw forgiveness. And screw backing off because she is crying. Little children cry and their mothers pick them up. But men who beat women don't care about tears. They tread right through that weak defense.

Stop because she is afraid? No. She is strong and capable of protecting herself and her family. She just doesn't know it yet.

"C'mon Beth. Don't let him get you this time. Keep your distance, then hit him." I say. The guys take my lead and begin to support her as well.

"You can do it."

"Kick him in the groin!"

Hal gives a crooked smile and says, "Hey now."

The mood lightens as she feels our support. He takes her to the ground again, but this time she scraps with him all the way down.

"Better. Now with Eric." I say stopping it.

The lightness disappears as she looks up. The familiarity of her friend and Sensei is gone. The suit steals his identity. He is every bully that ever pulled her long hair. He is holding the keys while the baby screams. He is standing over her while a crowd watches.

Eric grabs Beth by the shoulders. She hesitates and he comes in further. Now with his arms all the way around her, he lifts her and puts a knee on the ground at the same time. As they hit the ground she swears.

He lets go because he is a good guy. She gets to her feet and backs away. I put my hands on her back and push her toward Eric, saying, "Again." and "Don't be so nice Sensei."

She flashes me an angry look. Good! Angry is good. Angry people stand up for themselves. But she shouldn't have looked at me.

Eric seizes the opportunity to take a step and gain momentum. She kicks him on his way in but he doesn't feel a thing in the suit. The take-down is fast. I think, 'Nice job Sensei.'

Beth yells at him. It is not a word but it is full of rage. She thrusts a knee his way and he backs off slightly. Elbows and fists fly as she rises to her knees. I start to say, "Ya...."

And she is on her feet. Eric is slow to get up with the extra 40 pounds of suit. He is still on his hands and knees when she kicks him in the ribs.

"STOP!" I step in and put my body between them.

"Yeah! Kick him while he is down."

"Nice!"

The guys have no sympathy for Eric.

The tears on her face are just a habit now, they hold no power. I am crying too. I am so proud of this woman. No one will ever abuse her again. She just won't allow it.

CHAPTER 21 – SACRIFICE

"Shodan means, *first degree*, but in the Japanese tradition it symbolizes a boy becoming a man." Sensei John offered the first words of wisdom from the testing panel.

Sensei Hal added, "A very small group of people who train in martial arts will ever make it to black belt. It requires discipline, focus, continued effort, the ability to overcome and a willingness to change who you are over time."

Sensei Eric said, "If Jordan were here…It is a tradition to tell a new black belt that now he is ready to begin his true learning."

I add to Sensei Eric's words, "It is our honor to promote Jordan Brochu today to the rank of Shodan at Bushido Karate Dojo. He has earned the title of Senpai for his growth as a martial artist and as a person.

It was less than a year ago – the last time I saw Jordan. I was standing on the bottom step downstairs."

Prom had come and gone. He was no longer qualified to be a ward of the State and summer was ending. He had applied and been rejected by Navy, Air Force and Coast Guard.

"The Army had accepted his application and he was leaving. I hugged him and didn't want to let go. He was just days away from becoming a blue belt here at BKD, but life was taking a different direction." I paused to keep from crying.

"Jordan was killed in action by a roadside bomb in Afghanistan on August 31, 2009. We believe that his courage, dedication and ultimate sacrifice exemplify everything we believe to represent the black belt rank." I finished.

We placed his military photo on the wall and his black belt below it.

We honor his memory by telling his story to our students and wearing the belt.

CHAPTER 22 – NEVER GIVE UP

"Grab a partner." Steve is closest to Ian so they turn and face each other.

"Bow to your partner. Slow circular sparring. Nothing crazy, let's warm up." I say.

Steve is in close, closer than Ian likes, hanging on and striking in all the places people who follow rules don't go. Ian tries to back up, to get away but my kung fu friend is smooth and quick, anticipating his every move.

I let them go for a few minutes, then look at Hal and say, "You."

Hal is happy to receive Ian's kicks while he throws short quick jabs to the upper body and face. His love for boxing is never far away.

A few minutes later Hal is out and Alex is in.

Alex and Ian are the same height but Alex is 20 years older and 30 pounds heavier. The speed of youth and the power of weight even out the match up. They both love to kick to the head, but Ian is not used to fighting anyone with the same reach. Hands are moving, gear is necessary and everyone is smiling at the kicks they are trading; high, dangerous stuff with wings.

I move between Sensei Hal, and Sensei Eric. We stand in the classic black belt stance, arms crossed, feet shoulder width apart. My shoulder is solidly leaning against Eric's upper arm. He looks down at me when I flinch as Ian receives a fast punch to the face and says, "So much for slow."

I look at the guys, "Get the mats out." Alex, Hal and Steve move quickly to cover an area of the wood floor.

"Ian. Alex. On the mat."

I am standing behind Ian. Alex looks at me and I silently drop my chin acknowledging our plan. He attacks hard, fast, moving forward and punching. He steps back to create space for himself and his long leg extends out. Ian blocks the front kick but the punch gets in.

Ian's head moves back but he charges forward. He is courageous, stupid, but courageous.

Alex steps out of the way and catches Ian in a cheap shot as he goes by. He doesn't follow through, which would have been bad, but Ian is still stunned. Ian takes a big step forward and off the mat but pivots quickly. Using the momentum from the pivot he throws a wild hooking punch. Alex notices the punch, but only fast enough to move with it. This slight recovery gives Ian time to get his feet back under him.

A quick breath, feet set, guard up, Ian realizes the game has changed. In the midst of conflict Lizard brain only has two options: on or off. This feels real. This is real.

The fight evens out as Alex and Ian exchange blows for another 30 seconds.

"Yamae!" They keep at it.

"Stop!" Hal steps onto the mat between them.

"Alex. Off the mat. Hal, go."

Ian does a quick bow to Alex, then turns to Hal, bows and puts his guard back up.

There are no surprises this time, until I join the fight. Hal and I both attack.

I watch for that long kick, but Ian is conscious of the fight with me, having hurt me before. I didn't block and he didn't look before spinning 360 degrees and extending his left hand for a back fist. My jaw hurt for a month. Neither of us has forgotten.

I am his dojo mom and he is a respectful, homeschooled, Christian young man.

I tell the little kids (and Ian started when he was a little kid) that "You are responsible at all times and in all places for where your hands and feet end up."

But this is a black belt test. Hal and I escalate the fight. I am impressed with the skill it takes to be hard, fast and respectful. *Well done, Ian!*

Hal is a grappler and is good at getting people on the ground. We develop a pattern: Hal puts Ian on the floor, then I drive in as soon as he is standing, or not. Repeat.

Holy crap. This kid is just not getting tired.

I step off and put Steve and Eric on the mat with Ian.

He is wary of Eric's upper body reach and he is unsuccessfully trying to shake

off Steve. Steve is assaulting Ian's legs, pulling him to the ground in unpredictable ways.

Ian starts to falter. He takes a hard fall and looks shaken. Good. Finally.

"Stop!"

"Alex. Hal." Eric and Steve leave the mat.

Ian's face is a not great color.

I had a soccer coach who used to get upset with us for slide tackling too much, he would say, "It is exhausting to go to the ground so much. Stay on your feet!"

Alex and Hal have been resting. Ian has not. They trade shots and Ian goes to the ground, again. He gets up, and goes to the floor again.

Time slows down. I see Ian look up at Alex with a defeated expression, but in that instant something changes behind the mask. An intensity and a resolve appears that wasn't there a millisecond before. The difference between people and animals is that we negate our instincts for survival. Ian overrides this socialization and makes a choice.

From a crouching position he launches himself at the threat. Alex's solid stance is no match for Ian's momentum.

Ian wraps his arms around Alex's waist and they fly across the mat.

They are still in the air when the word begins to pass my lips, "Yamae!"

There is no telling where this will go if I let it continue.

We erupt with applause. Eric lends a hand to Alex as they untangle themselves to get up.

That was his moment, the test. It didn't come from us. It never comes from the testing panel. It is the manifestation of the visceral human response of sensing life in danger.

It is something you unleash, not knowing you were capable of such an action, not knowing the depth of your survival instinct until it is brought forth. It is an untapped well, once discovered, there for you to draw upon for the rest of your life.

Ian brought his work ethic to college. His confidence will be at the foundation of every job interview. He will be a compassionate and amazing dad, but that is his family's doing. And we will always be proud to call him a black belt at BKD.

There is no mystique to being a black belt, just hard work. Show up for class, even when you don't feel like it. Put yourself in the fight, regardless of the potential for loss. Obstacles? What obstacles? Go around. Go over, or punch through. When exhaustion clouds your judgment, trust your instincts and attack.

ABOUT THE AUTHOR

I live in the "village" of Casco, Maine with my husband, Eric, two kids: Jordan and Nick, and LabraChow Sadie. I am blessed to walk barefoot, or in my LLBean slippers, to the dojo from my kitchen in all sorts of weather.

Simon Sinek inspired me to ask, "Why…Why karate?" The answer: Because karate made me a better person. My mission is to Make Better People.

The dojo is my home and I am immersed in karate. It defines me, surrounds me and travels with me always. I tell my instructors that the most important thing that we do is to connect with our students.
It is our core philosophy.

I jokingly say that my title, Renshi, means wicked good teacher.
Translated it means polished or master instructor.
Renshi is also a style of Japanese Poetry. It is collaborative in nature, based in tradition but willing to break the rules. I like that.

This process of writing has been reflective and revealing, as if I had asked the question, 'Lisa—What do you believe?'

I found out that I believe in people. I believe that struggle leads to victory. I believe that the most difficult students are my greatest teachers.
I believe that the martial arts are an
incredible vehicle for personal growth and discovery.

I believe that every person should find that thing that they just cannot live without, and pursue it with passion.

Yours in Bushido,

Renshi Lisa Magiera

Made in the USA
Middletown, DE
21 April 2017